D0462385

.G

The Complete Guide to Lightweight Travel

by Barbara DesChamps

To the Hansens,
May all your travels be
relaxing & rewarding!
Barbara

Château Publishing
Nevada City,
California

IT'S IN THE BAG
The Complete Guide to Lightweight Travel
by Barbara DesChamps

Published by:
Château Publishing
Post Office Box 2401
Nevada City, CA 95959
U.S.A.

Publisher's Cataloging-in-Publication Data

DesChamps, Barbara
It's In The Bag: The Complete Guide to Lightweight Travel
112 p. 22cm.
ISBN 0-9710525-0-6
1. Travel – Guidebooks
2. Travel – Equipment
3. Travel – Clothing and Accessories
4. Travel – Health
I. Title
910.202—dc21

Library of Congress Catalog Number: 2001126782

Acknowledgements

The author wishes to thank the following people for their artistic contributions: Neil Huddleson, who produced all the black and white photographs for the book; Matthias Schossig of iTRANSmedia, who did the typesetting layout; Anne Adden, of Maverick Designs, who helped with the cover layout; Brian Goggin, who graciously allowed us to use a photograph of "SAMSON", a site specific sculpture he created for the Sacramento International Airport, and Jacques Louis David (1748-1825) for his portrait of Madame Récamier, which he began in 1800, but never completed. David was the first director of the Louvre Museum, and the painting hangs there. For our cover illustration, we have added some details which David never got around to.

DISCLAIMER

This book is intended to provide information which can help the traveler to choose luggage and equipment. A sampling of rules and regulations is included to give readers an idea of the type of restrictions they may encounter. Airline policies and government regulations can change overnight. Readers are encouraged to check with their airlines and the appropriate government agencies for up-to-the-minute information.

The listing in this book of sources for equipment and information does not imply any endorsement or recommendation of any product or service. No one has paid to be listed. The publisher and author shall have neither liability nor responsibility to any person or entity with respect to any loss or damage caused, or alleged to have been caused, directly or indirectly, by the information contained in this book.

CONTENTS

Chapter One

FLY THROUGH THE AIR WITH THE GREATEST OF EASE

Advantages of Lightweight Travel

As early nomads contemplated their moves, one question loomed large: How do we take everything we need, without weighing ourselves down? 200,000 years later, more or less, jet-age travelers ask themselves the same question. Here, finally, gathered together in one place, is everything you ever wanted to know, and probably more, about traveling lightly.

Recently, I heard that airlines are losing 7,000 bags per day. The first time I flew on a commercial airline, in 1969, it mis-routed my checked suitcase, and didn't deliver it to me until the day I returned home. Fortunately, it was a short trip, I had a small carry-on case with toiletries and underwear, and I was able to borrow a suit from my aunt. I was lucky. Some luggage disappears into a black hole, never to be seen again by its owner. It's been said that there are two types of luggage: Carry-on and Lost. Over the years I have refined my system so that I can fit everything I need, even for a long trip, in one small, lightweight bag that fits under an airline seat. With the aid of this book, you can do the same. There will be exceptions, of course. If you are going to a very cold, snowy location, or have to carry heavy equipment along, you may have to check a bag. But I still urge you to carry with you the essential, valuable, and hard-to-replace items. The alternative may be an unhappy vacation.

Here are some more reasons to stick with carry-on luggage: There is a ceiling on what airlines will pay for lost or damaged luggage, and for international flights, that ceiling is very low. They will pay only the depreciated value, not the replacement value. You have to supply receipts to back up your claim, which is impossible with dozens of small items. You will not be reimbursed for the time it takes to find all those items again, probably many days. You may have to fill out forms twice: Once when the bag first goes missing, and again when it is "officially" lost. Expect to have to argue with the airline over the value of your stuff, and don't expect payment for a couple of months.

You may have to bring all your luggage to the counter (no curbside checking) as a security measure, especially for international flights. The lines are often long and slow. You may have to go through customs (with all bags) between two legs of your flight, and then carry everything to check in for the connection. Checking bags to the final destination may eliminate this extra carrying, but increase the risk of loss.

At many major airports, there are fast trains or shuttles to the city center which are much cheaper than taxis, but it is difficult to use them if you are loaded with lots of luggage. You can move more quickly with just a carry-on, and be a less likely target for thieves and scam artists. In many places, cabs can levy an extra charge for each bag. If you are traveling with companions on business, and they do not check luggage, they aren't going to be happy about waiting at the airport for 45 minutes or so for your luggage to appear.

Many well-traveled people have systems for getting by with one bag and you can read brief sections about that in other books. They mostly deal with clothing, and leave out all the little items that can help your trip run smoothly. Their theory is that you can buy whatever else you need along the way. Aside from the fact that you can't find everything in every location, there is the matter of time and convenience. Do you really want to spend hours of your valuable vacation time searching for a small item that you could have packed at home? Considering that you might be spending hundreds of dollars per day for your vacation, it isn't likely.

The checklists in this book (alone worth the price of admission) have been developed during three decades of overseas travel (and a few backpacking trips) by someone who is a compulsive organizer. The checklists are exhaustive, so you won't forget anything. When you see them, your first thought may well be: "No way is all that stuff going to fit in a small bag." Well, it depends. You should not need every item on each trip, especially items on the Miscellany list. If you miniaturize everything possible (explained in Chapter three,) most items will fit. If you also share items with your travel companion, they will definitely fit. I don't mean sharing your toothbrush, but there are more than 40 items on the lists which are sharable. For each trip, copy the lists, cross out the items you won't need, and use the modified lists as an aid in shopping and packing.

The travel suggestions in this book are applicable whether you are going to Boston, Berlin or Bangkok, on business or for pleasure. Many people think that a cruise requires more clothing than other vacations because the same fellow passengers will be seeing them everyday, and some formal attire may also be necessary. But please consider that if your luggage doesn't arrive by sailing time, your shopping options on board are much more limited than they would be on land. You might find a fancy dress, but not a good fitting bra or shoe. It's better to take a carry-on bag and supplement with a checked bag, which might not even be necessary if you follow the tips in the wardrobe chapter.

Many people buy special padded cases for their laptop computers, but these are targets for thieves. If your trip is not long, try packing the laptop in the middle of your carry-on bag, with your clothes on both sides as padding. Actually, if you are the only one handling the bag, padding may not be necessary.

Currently, airlines do not allow sharp metal items in carry-on luggage, not even hair pins! You can pack them in a small corrugated box, labeled with your name and destination address, and check it. If it is lost, you can apply for reimbursement for these easily replaced items, and keep everything else in your carry-on.

For luggage which may be checked, make sure it is sturdy enough to survive the baggage handling systems, but not expensive looking. Do not pack valuable items such as money, jewelry, cameras, or negotiable securities. Do not pack irreplaceable items. Do not pack glass containers. Plastic bottles should go in plastic bags, because they often leak a little with changes in air pressure. One woman told of shampoo leaking onto sanitary supplies, and finding replacements in Moscow to be quite primitive. Do not pack perishables: Consider the consequences of smelly cheese or rotten meat if your bag is delayed. Do not pack in checked luggage anything you absolutely must have for your trip. If any item is at all breakable, you should wrap it with lots of padding and put it in a hard case or heavy duty box, just as though you were mailing it. Choose the cheapest, least important items for checked luggage, and the luggage is more likely to arrive with you at your destination. However, unless you are cruising or renting one car for your entire vacation, try to stick to one bag. The basic rule is: You should be able to carry all your luggage, even for a kilometer (over one half mile.) You may have to.

It's In The Bag

"Samson"
A site specific sculpture by Brian Goggin
for the Sacramento International Airport

Chapter Two

PAPA'S GOT A BRAND NEW BAG

Choosing the Right Luggage

You've probably seen them at airports: The people with too much luggage. They carry large shoulder bags, sling garment bags over their backs, and try to drag along yet more in small wheeled bags which are awkward on curbs or steps. Did you ever wonder how they make quick flight connections, or board small ferry boats? The answer is: Not very well. For them, getting there is not half the fun, nor is it fun for the rest of us when the overly endowed (with luggage) try to carry their embarrassment of riches on board the aircraft, and stuff the excess into the overhead bins. This puts some real wrinkles in your coat and hat, and poses serious safety problems if the latches are not perfect. I've heard of people putting bowling balls up there, but even a heavy bag could do you in. Aircraft boarding takes twice as long as it should because of all the jockeying for storage space. Some travel writers even advise people on tricks to smuggle more on board! Fortunately, some of the airlines are getting wise.

Some airlines limit you to one bag which can fit under the seat in front of yours. If you're facing the bulkhead, you're out of luck, so reserve a different seat. Generally, the dimensions of the bag cannot exceed 9" x 14" x 22" (cm: about 23 x 35 x 56) and some carriers have little cages at the gate to test your bag. If it doesn't fit, it's no go. Outside the U.S., some airlines are even more strict, so if you can get by with a smaller bag, so much the better. An 18 inch bag is sometimes recommended, but may be too small for most people, and not easy to come by. I own bags in the 19 to 20 inch range. Some commuter type aircraft are pretty tight. With a soft bag packed not too fully, you probably can squeeze it in. In flight, you can remove your shoes and put your feet on the bag. This has become a necessity with the short legroom in coach class. If you have really long legs, you might have to give up on the idea of carry-on luggage, or upgrade to business or first class.

British Airways has a 6 kg or 13 lb. limit for carry-ons, and their agent may not tell you this when you book your flight. You will find out at the airport when they take your soft, squishy bag and throw it in the hold with the hard cases. Ouch! You might be able to meet their weight limit on a short trip to a warm place. My solution is not to fly British Airways, and always to ask other airline agents about their luggage restrictions. Although baggage allowances in the U.S. are fairly liberal, within Europe you may be limited to 20 kg or 44 lb., including checked baggage. Your carry-on will probably weigh less than half of that.

Other limitations vary by airline and country. Sometimes you are allowed to carry on two bags, sometimes only one.

In general, most airlines will count the following items as a bag: Briefcase, camera bag, tote bag or backpack. In general, most airlines don't count the following items as a bag: Small purse or waistpack, small camera, laptop computer, overcoat, umbrella, hat, binoculars, canes, crutches, walkers, and collapsible wheelchairs. Also generally allowed are infant necessities, including seat and collapsible stroller. Some airlines allow other items too, but commuter airlines may not have enough space, and may "gate check" some items. If in doubt about an item, ask the reservation agent.

If you know that you are never going to check your luggage, you should look for a bag that is very lightweight. I have an old one that weighs just 1 kg or 2.2 lb. empty, because it is very plain. I have a newer one which is 1.825 kg or about 4 lbs. It has a sturdier fabric, more zippered sections, and a shoulder strap. If you add extra compartments, extra zippers, backpack straps or wheels to luggage, it gets heavier. The backpack or shoulder straps have the advantage of leaving your hands free. I would try to avoid the other doodads. If the bag is lightweight, you don't need wheels, which, along with handle and stiffened frame, make the bag heavy. Wheels will not help much on stairs, or when you are jumping onto the small ferry boat. Unfortunately, the manufacturers are making more "wheel-ons" than carry-ons. When you find a lightweight bag, it is often not the regulation size. See the Sources chapter for carry-on bags and backpacks.

Children should carry back-packs. Their arm muscles have not yet developed through years of hard work, and you don't want to throw their spines out of alignment either. Their packs should not be too heavy because the adults will carry most miscellaneous items.

Canvas is sturdy, but cannot be wiped clean and may not be a good choice in wet weather. The tougher, water-resistant nylons are better. Try to pick something in a dark, solid color. A flashy or expensive-looking bag will attract unwanted attention from thieves and customs agents. However, a bag color that matches or harmonizes with your travel wardrobe can look very classy, and might even help you get favorable treatment, as explained in the Wardrobe chapter.

Two men went on a two night business trip. One took a 29 inch suitcase, which he checked. The second put a clean shirt, socks and undies in a compartment of his attaché case, which he carried, of course. Each thought the other an extremist. In fact, most people could get by with a smaller bag than they thought possible, and many bags advertized as "overnighters" or "weekenders" will hold everything you need for a trip lasting months.

A clerk in a luggage store told me about a woman who asked for a set of the largest suitcases they had, and this was for a short vacation. When the clerk inquired how the woman was going to carry all that weight, the woman blythely replied: "Oh, my husband will carry it." Even if her husband is a professional weight lifter, I pity him. You should be able to keep your packed bag under 10 kg or 22 lbs. The rest of this book tells you how.

Chapter Three

HONEY, I SHRUNK THE KIT

The Art of Miniaturization

There is an episode of the PBS series "Mister Bean" which shows him preparing to take a trip with a very small suitcase. He cuts off the legs of some slacks, only to find that he already has some shorts waiting to be packed. He briefly considers amputating the limbs of his "Teddy" but cannot "bear" to do it. He squeezes most of the toothpaste into the sink so the tube will be smaller. I am not going to suggest that you follow his examples. My tricks will not be as humorous, and your bag will not be as small, but the idea is the same: To fit everything you need into that one bag.

To what extent should you miniaturize? Rick Steves, who created the Travels in Europe series for PBS, advises you to take just enough supplies to get started, and then buy a tube of what you think is toothpaste in some little town. I'm pretty careful since I had an allergic reaction to a major brand in the U.S., and some toothpaste ingredients are unhealthy. Most places in Europe will have something acceptable; many places on this globe will not. Also, please remember that Rick goes to Europe for several months at a time, in order to prepare and film his shows, so he is bound to run out of something sooner or later. When the lighting is bad for filming, he has plenty of time to shop around and restock his supplies. You may only have two or four weeks; do you want to spend a chunk of it shopping for toiletries?

Consider your individual circumstance. If you are taking a short vacation, a sample size will do. If you are going for two months, which is typical for me, you can plan ahead. When your large tube of toothpaste or sunscreen has at least enough left in it for two months, set it aside with your travel stuff, and start a new tube for home use. If you write down the date in your calendar or on a piece of paper in the toothpaste drawer, you can keep track of how long the 6 or 7 ounce tube of toothpaste lasts.

I kept track of my shampoo usage, and it was a lot more than you would believe. I'll take plenty if space allows. You'll have to do your own calculations. For shorter trips (or shorter hair) you can put shampoo in a smaller plastic bottle. Better hotels often provide tiny packets of shampoo: OK if you don't need much and you aren't picky. I sometimes use that to wash nylons.

There are small covers for the bristle end of the toothbrush. These take up less space and weight than a full-size holder, and are also more likely to work with the curved handle brushes. You might only need a 20 yard package of dental floss instead of the 100 yard size. Look for smaller sizes of everything. Some drug and grocery stores have a section with trial sizes. Convenience stores, often associated with service stations, usually have a variety of products in small sizes for the traveler. Another good reason for calling some of them mini-marts!

Each item you miniaturize saves only a little weight and space, but after 40 items or so, it adds up to considerable savings. Miniaturization is especially important with your day pack, so the items on that list should be given the highest priority. Gradually, as time permits, tackle the other items. Travelers often compete to find the smallest version of an item that still works properly.

Skin lotions and similar items can go in small bottles or jars. When I finish a nice, small container at home, I wash and save it, so I have an assortment for trips of different lengths. Don't buy products in aerosol cans; the added propellant makes them bulky. It's also a bad idea to pack them if there is a chance that your bag may be checked. Aerosol cans may explode in the lower air pressure of the cargo hold.

Now we come to a dicey proposition, regarding what I call the pharmacy or medicine kit. It is generally recommended that you NOT separate pills or capsules from their original containers. You might be accused of drug smuggling and go to jail. Having warned you of that, I will admit that I miniaturize my stash of vitamins, minerals, and herbal remedies to the greatest extent physically possible. You can read all about it in the Pharmacy chapter. I hope you never read about it in the newspaper.

Once you've acquired tiny versions of everything possible, how do you keep them from getting lost in the bottom of your luggage? The answer is to group them in clear plastic bags, which allow you to see the contents easily and may speed up airport inspections. Drugstores often have clear toiletries bags. For less money, grocery stores have freezer bags. The zippered kind come in different sizes to fit your needs: Sandwich (about 6" x 6"), Quart (7" x 8"), and Gallon (about 11" x 11"). They are also good for laundry bags, either before washing, or after (if your clothes didn't dry completely overnight,) for wet swimsuits, and dusty sandals. If your shampoo bottle leaks a little, it's in the bag. You could also use plain plastic bags with twist ties or rubber bands. The bags can be washed and dried easily, but take along extra. They are cheap, lightweight, and handy for all sorts of things, including ice packs if you suffer a sprained ankle.

Miniaturization has a long history. In the 19th century, many gentlemen had "necessary kits" which were small cylindrical containers with tiny tools such as fruit knives. Perhaps these gave someone the idea for the first "Swiss Army" type knife. You can get eight great weeks' worth of necessities in that itty-bitty bag, if you miniaturize everything possible.

Chapter Four

RUB A DUB DUB, THREE KITS IN A TUB

Clean Up with the Basin, Shower and Laundry Kits

Most of these items are things you use every day, but some may be new to you. Some basins are missing drain plugs. It could be that someone took them, but it is also likely that the hotel is trying to discourage you from using a lot of water, especially in doing hand laundry. You can easily get around this problem by using your own universal drain plug, which is simply a thin, flexible disc of rubber or vinyl, about 5" or 13 cm in diameter. It is held in place at first by your hand, and then by the weight of water above it. It works pretty well as long as you don't shove it to the side while swishing your socks. If you can't find one, you can make one yourself. I cut down a jar lid opener.

A hair snare is an item of similar material and dimension with a raised center portion riddled with holes. Put it over the sink, shower or bathtub drain to avoid clogging it when washing your hair. It also keeps long hair from sliding down the sink drain. If you need to clean your home drains frequently, then you should use this gizmo so you and subsequent hotel guests will not be ankle-deep in scummy water. If the drain does back up, you can always point to the hair snare and say: "I didn't do it."

Another handy gadget is a spray attachment with a hose which connects to the sink or tub spout depending on adaptor. This can be a big help if you need to wash your hair where there is no shower, or for rinsing your slacks in the tub. This takes up a lot more space than the drain covers, and is therefore optional.

Our Istanbul hotel had a lovely marble bathroom, but the hand shower had a very wide spray pattern, inefficient for rinsing. Each night, we substituted our own spray attachment, and then re-installed theirs before housekeeping came in the next day.

Self-service laundromats are showing up in more and more places, but I suggest you not rely on them. They can be harsh on your clothes, and the hotter-than-home dryers may shrink them. A hotel washing machine is good for some items, and the spin cycle should eliminate dripping. If you follow the suggestions in the Wardrobe section of this book, you should be able to wash all items easily by hand. Laundry liquid is far preferable to hand soap, which can build up a residue in your clothes, especially in hard water. Powder detergent will not dissolve easily, and will not work for pre-treating problem areas.

It's difficult to figure usage with so many variables like water hardness, amount of soil, and detergent concentration. A good estimate would be one pint or 0.5 l per person for six weeks. Unfortunately, most detergent comes in very large bottles. One "cold water wash" is available in a pint bottle, but it costs as much as three liters of the other products, and I don't think it works any better. I fill an empty shampoo bottle with my usual brand and label it clearly. For a long trip, where extra bulk and weight could be a problem, this would be the first place to cut back, and just take one bottle, because you can buy more for a refill at almost any store, and give the rest to the cleaning staff. You may even find some nifty products abroad. I bought a tube of white stuff in Germany which was designed primarily to treat collars, but could also be used for general washing. (Note to Rick Steves: It wasn't toothpaste.)

The biggest laundry problem involves a place to hang the dripping clothes. You DON'T want to risk water damage. The best place to hang is from the towel racks that some better hotels have over the end of the tub. The next best is a built-in clothesline over the tub. Bare-bones hotels probably have neither. Small items like nylon stockings, socks, and bikinis can be blotted half dry with a towel and hung almost anywhere. However, bare metal hangers can cause permanent rust spots on your clothes. Plastic hangers are more likely to pass airport inspection than vinyl coated metal, but are more bulky. Wooden clothespins are also made in a small size, about 1 3/4" or 45 mm. Look for these in craft stores. Some people use safety pins (rustproof, I hope) but they slide around. Others use braided clothesline without pins, but this doesn't work well for larger items such as skirts, slacks and shirts. Figure a dozen pins and three or four hangers per person. The toothbrush is for scrubbing areas such as shirt underarms and collars (works as a nailbrush too.) The gloves protect your hands from detergent. I use them for shampooing also.

Some Bed and Breakfast owners will let you hang laundry on their outdoor clothesline, but ask ahead. Before committing to a stay in Cambridge, we asked, and the woman said no, it caused dampness. Evidently, tourists are causing the famous British fog.

Wash a couple of pairs of socks and undies whenever you get the chance. Then, once or twice a week, stay in a better hotel where you can wash a few shirts and a pair of slacks, and hang them above the tub. Do not wring, and smooth away any folds. Such items will take longer to dry, so try to wash them before dinner. If they still aren't dry by morning, and you are not staying a second night, here are some options: A hair dryer or travel iron may finish the drying process, but these are heavy items you may not want to take. You can put damp clothes in a plastic bag and hang them at the next hotel (they shouldn't be dripping anymore.) If you have a car, you can hang slightly damp items or lay them on a cleaned back seat.

For your basin kit, you may prefer to use a heavier duty holder, which is more likely to stay upright on the counter or shelf than a plastic freezer bag. Try to find the clear plastic ones with stiffening in the base, often available in drugstores. Of course you will want to miniaturize the contents: Half ounce sticks of antiperspirant; 30 cotton swabs instead of 300. Put a thin wash cloth in a sandwich bag; not all hotels supply them. The plastic cup may also be used in the shower. Items like these can be moved around as needed, and stored in whichever kit is convenient. If you have a lot of make-up or other items, you might add a second, smaller bag. Disposable razors are lightweight, and unlikely to chip the basin. Keep any extras with the miscellaneous items.

Remember that, even if you start out with five pounds of shampoo, conditioner, and laundry detergent, by the end of the trip there should be very little remaining. You can leave it for the housekeeping staff and have more room for your purchases.

Some people keep toiletries and pharmacy kits filled up and ready to go, so they can travel on very short notice. This would also be helpful if your neighborhood were evacuated in an emergency.

Contents of kits displayed

Chapter Five

HOME AWAY FROM HOME REMEDIES

Your Own Private Pharmacy

People have gotten into serious trouble when unidentified substances were found in their possession. There was even an instance when inspectors found grains of sand in a toiletry kit, left over from a beach vacation, and thought "crystal meth." It is always recommended that medicines (especially prescriptions) be in their original containers with labels. Anything strange or narcotic should be accompanied by the doctor's prescription. Some countries, like Greece, don't even allow codeine.

Most prescription bottles are small, but this is not true of vitamins and minerals. If you take a one per day type, you can just buy the smallest bottle that will take you through your vacation. I, on the other hand, take a custom mix of nine products, and they don't all come in small bottles. When my trip is short, I group them in small plastic bags for each use. On longer trips, I figure how many I'll need of each, and put them into the smallest plastic bottle or jar that will hold them. I label everything. No official has ever looked at my "stash," but if one does, I hope he believes that those capsules are really just calcium and other minerals. Being a middle-aged woman means I don't fit the smuggler profiles. If you are closer to twenty years old, you may not want to use my system, but then, you probably aren't taking calcium capsules.

You don't want to search for an all-night pharmacy in a strange city. If you're not feeling well, you don't want to go to one during the day either. Prepared with a reasonable assortment of the most common remedies, you probably won't need to. There is actually a higher probability that you will get sick during a trip than during the same time interval at home. There are several reasons for this. You will be exposed to viruses and bacteria that have not been to your home, and you have little or no immunity to them. Colds you get abroad may hit harder.

Airlines recirculate as much air as they can for fuel economy, because bringing in a lot of fresh air through the engines causes a loss in power. Then that air has to be warmed, requiring more energy, so airlines try to get by with less. The recycled air is filtered, but some people believe that it still has a higher than normal concentration of microbes. You probably won't get much sleep on the airplane: It's cramped, and someone nearby is sure to be shuffling cards or talking loudly through the night. Jet lag is a problem made worse by lack of sleep on the airplane. You can have problems with other forms of transport: Frequently, you can't change your seat to get away from that coughing child who doesn't use a handkerchief.

No one can guarantee that any municipal water system will always be safe; wells or streams can become contaminated by accident. Bottled water is usually the best bet. In areas where this is not available, you may need to filter the water and/or purify it with chemicals. Traditionally, chlorine or iodine have been used, and you can use liquid or tablets. You should give the chemicals 30 minutes to do their work. The water won't taste good, but this is an incentive not to drink too much of the unhealthy concoction.

Recently, I have heard and read testimonials about Grapefruit Seed Extract, or GSE. It is said to be more effective than chlorine or iodine against a variety of micro-organisms, and at a lower concentration, down to ten parts per million. At this rate, you can just discern a slight bitterness, and no odor. People are also claiming that, at higher concentrations, it can un-do the damage from drinking untreated water! Some also claim that it is effective externally against fungal and other infections. I can't vouch for any of this except the taste test; you'll need to read the literature and make up your own mind. Remember that, even if the microbes are killed, you still need to consider other forms of pollution. If downstream from industry, I prefer bottled water.

Even if you stick to bottled water, there is a chance you could get some intestinal distress from food. It's a good idea to carry anti-diarrheal medicine, in case the problem persists for more than one day. Loperamide tablets are better than the heavy, liquid stuff. In case of allergies or a cold, you may want a decongestant and/or antihistamine. Goldenseal may help to fight an infection. Zinc lozenges and echinacea may help you ward off that cold. If you are prone to motion sickness, you may need ginger capsules or some drugstore preventative or the special wristbands with buttons. A few cough drops are a good idea, to tide you over until you can buy a bottle of cough medicine, which is too big to carry "just-in-case." You may want to add a trial size of Acetaminophen or Ibuprofen. Some products come in a foil blister pack. Instead of taking the whole box, you can cut out a section of one sheet. These are usually labeled, but if not, cut out the part of the box which tells what it contains, and attach the two with a rubber band. Since pills and capsules are so tiny, they are worth carrying.

The rest depends on your particular circumstances. If insect bites or poison oak or ivy cause you a reaction, a small tube of cortisone cream is in order. If you are going to be hiking in a swampy area, an anti-fungal medicine for your feet is the thing.

If you will be traveling to a very remote area, you might want to have prescription antibiotic pills with you. In places with pharmacies, just the written prescription should be sufficient. For mountain trekking, an elastic bandage might be needed, along with a good first aid kit. In areas with pharmacies, a few adhesive bandages and a small amount of moleskin are probably enough. Put all your pharmacy items together in one or two bags. If there are no liquid items, you can use a cloth kit.

Everything shown fits in the carry-on bag.

Chapter Six

WHATEVER GETS YOU THROUGH THE DAY

Your Day Pack and Money Belt

Your day pack is your home away from hotel room or car, and should contain everything you need until nightfall. It can be a purse with a shoulder strap that you wear bandolier style, a waist pack, or a small back pack. I've tried them all and the waist pack wins hands down (and hands free.) The purse puts a kink in your neck and shoulder, and the back pack is uncomfortable in warm weather, which is when you're most likely to travel. Gather all your tiny items together, grouped together in sandwich bags, and then buy a waist pack which will hold them.

Some people prefer to wear a fishing vest or, in cooler weather, a jacket with lots of pockets. For more security, you can wear the vest inside-out, or sew large pockets to the inside of the jacket. These options are convenient, but may give you a lumpy appearance. I've tried putting everything in the pockets of a parka; after a couple of hours, my shoulders hurt.

Take one or two little wet-naps for clean-ups, or even better, put some liquid soap in a teeny squeeze container, like the ones used for contact lens wetting solution. This will take up less room in the long run. If you need to wash more than your hands, use a clean handkerchief with soap and water, and then return it to its sandwich bag. Take only enough vitamins and other pills for the day, and use the smallest pillboxes that will hold them. Ditto for gum, mints, or lozenges. Two safety pins and adhesive bandages will probably be enough. Take a small emery board for nicked fingernails.

If you expect mosquitos, take a one ounce stick or bottle of repellant, not a spray can. I like the stick (made by Cutter) but it's difficult to find. If you want to take perfume along, you can find some packaged like a ball-point pen (can't be spilled.) For shopping, I take a one meter tape measure which has inches on the other side and is only 1.5 inches (less than 4 cm) square. You will need a coin purse (or two if you are going back and forth between two countries) and just enough cash for small outlays such as museum admission, bus tickets and lunch.

On the subject of food, you may want to take some compact nutrition like nuts and dried fruit. This is a very good idea on the airplane too. We were once stuck on the runway for hours during a lightning storm, and they could not serve food while waiting for clearance to take off. Do not take peanuts on the airplane however. Some people have a life-threatening allergic reaction to just the odor of them, which will travel throughout the plane. One of the most important things you can carry is water. The easiest way is in a mesh bag with a shoulder strap which can hold a bottle up to 1.5 liters. Refer to the Day Pack checklist for other items you may need. Also, items such as picnic gear from the Miscellany list may occasionally go in the day pack.

I'VE GOT YOU NEXT TO MY SKIN: Some items that you would normally carry in a wallet are missing from the Day Pack list. That is because they belong in your money belt instead. Get one large enough to hold your passport, driver's license, travelers' cheques, credit cards, and excess cash (is there such a thing?) from the most recent cheque. If your trip is long, take mostly $500 cheques; in the old days, we were stuck with $100s and they were bulky on long trips. Take a few $100s and/or $50s for transactions with merchants. Some of them actually prefer dollars and won't charge you more than the bank rate or commission, but you need to compare. Some people find it useful to carry some $1 and $5 bills for taxis and tips before they cash a travelers' cheque. Be aware that they won't always be accepted abroad, and using them in some places is illegal.

Two separate credit card accounts are better than one. Some rental car companies and hotels place a "hold" on part of your credit limit, and may max it out. Then you can use the second card for other things. With two people, each carries one card. Although an ATM card is convenient and gives you a better exchange rate than a travelers' cheque, it doesn't have the fraud protection of a credit card. Thieves have been known to kidnap people and force them to withdraw two daily limits, one before midnight and one after. They can also steal the card and use it as they would a credit card at retail stores. A new invention is the AAA Global Currency card (see Sources chapter.) They say it has the same fraud protection as a VISA credit card.

The money belt is also the place for your personal telephone calling card if you choose to take it, so no one will run up your home telephone account (the inexpensive Fone Card you can buy in most places can go in the day pack) and a road service card. This last can be used with other auto clubs which have reciprocal agreements with yours, to get good maps and other information. It may also be good for some hotel and rental car discounts.

We spent a long and lovely day in Naples, walking many miles. We decided to take a bus back to the train station so we could "Return to Sorrento" and our hotel. The bus was packed, just the place for pickpockets. My husband had a thin wallet in his front slacks pocket and pressed his hand against it tightly as he descended from the bus, preventing its loss from a strong tug. We examined it that night and saw a tiny pin hole. We laughed. Even if the thief's hook had worked, the wallet contained only a small amount of money. Our dinner money and credit card were in our money belts, the rest of our stash in the hotel safe.

If you are going out at night, you might want to leave your passport at the hotel desk; the hotel usually keeps it the first night anyway. Carry one credit card and a small amount of cash for the evening.

Paper items should go in sandwich bags, so as not to be degraded by perspiration. I wear the money belt under my shirt, with the bulky part in the back, but some might like to wear it over their shirt in front, just below the belt. Factor in the extra bulk when choosing your wardrobe.

If you go swimming, what do you do with your valuables? Here is one solution I have read but not tried. Put your moneybelt and keys in a sealed plastic bag. Put the bag in a watertight security wallet or camera pouch, and incorporate some air before you seal it so it will float. Attach it to your swimsuit securely, so your hands are free.

If you want to carry a camera, I recommend you buy the cheap one ($5 to $10) that you turn in for processing. Losing one is not a big deal, and no one is going to steal it unless you've been taking pictures of military installations, which is usually forbidden anyway. Tourists have suffered serious injuries when they were mugged simply for their expensive cameras. Before wasting film at a tourist site, check out the postcards, which are cheaper and better, because they are shot when the lighting is optimum. Don't shoot people, unless they really want you to. A camera can make people feel like objects, and be a barrier to friendship.

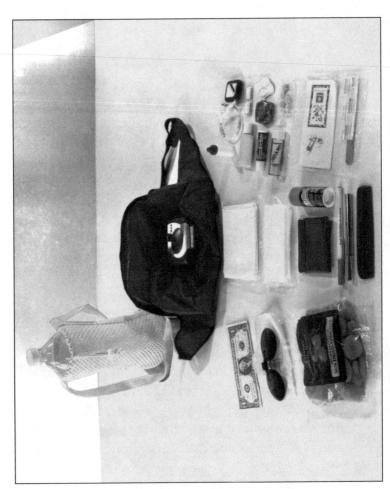

Day pack contents and water bottle holder

Chapter Seven

A TICKET TO RIDE

Paperwork To Go

In addition to airline tickets and other travel passes, each person in your group should have complete reservation information in case you get separated. Include the name, address, and phone number of the first night's hotel so you can meet there.

Your passport should be safe in your money belt, but just in case, take a photocopy of the name page to make replacement easier. According to the U.S. State Department, more than 30,000 U.S. passports are lost or stolen each year. When crossing borders and going through airport customs, it is easier to carry the passport in your bag, but keep your eye on the bag. The passport is a tempting target for people wishing to enter your country.

You may want to take extra photos for on-the-spot visas. One woman told me of her experience entering Nepal. She didn't have a photo for the visa, but another woman had an extra and gave it to her. Even though the hair color was different, the officials didn't question it. Perhaps to them, all Westerners look alike.

Take copies of any prescriptions, including those for eyeglasses. If you can't get by without your glasses for a few days, you must take a back-up, perhaps your previous pair. You will want either a tiny address book or just a printout of the people you might want to contact. Include a small amount of lightweight paper and envelopes for those times when a postcard is not enough.

Depending on your destinations, you may need an International Certificate of Vaccination, and it is wise to get your shots and pills well before your trip. Regarding vaccinations, there are those required by a country to protect its own citizens, and then there are those you may want to protect yourself. Ask your local health department, the CENTERS FOR DISEASE CONTROL in Atlanta, GA 30333 (www.cdc.gov) or check the U.S. State Department travel advisories. Countries with health problems do not like to advertise them; it's bad for the tourist business.

In 1979, we spent the month of September in Great Britain. We saw that a lot of people had bad coughs, but when we questioned them about the reason, they were not very forthcoming. We caught that "British" cough, and suffered with it through the month of October in France, and for a while after. It did not respond to antibiotics or cough medicines. We wondered why two formerly very healthy people couldn't seem to shake it for six weeks. It was years later that we discovered there had been an epidemic of whooping cough in Great Britain during most of 1979, but it was kept as quiet as possible. The doctors in France knew nothing about it. It was also news to our local health department that our childhood vaccinations did not confer lifetime immunity.

An International Driver's Permit is necessary in some countries, and may be useful in others. It might provide temporary ID within a country if your passport is lost or stolen. For full time students, an International Student Identity Card can provide lots of discounts. THE COUNCIL ON INTERNATIONAL EDUCATION EXCHANGE is at 205 East 42nd St., New York, NY 10017, 1-800-438-2643. Keep a list of credit card and travelers' cheques numbers in a separate location. Before leaving the U.S., get Customs certificates of registration for your foreign made items, or they will be subject to duty when you return. For maps, you will generally find a better selection and lower prices in your destination cities. Try the book and stationery stores; gas stations don't seem to carry much. Many tourist offices hand out city maps at little or no cost. If you are visiting less-developed areas, buy ahead. If backpacking in the U.S., go to a Geological Survey Office, or try a map and blueprint company in the vicinity of your destination.

If you are a member of an auto club such as AAA, some national auto clubs have reciprocal agreements. I took a tram to the ELPA office in Athens, showed my AAA card, and was given a good road map of Greece, much better than the one Hertz gave me later with my rental car. The helpful staff also plied me with brochures.

Guide books enable you to get the most out of your trip, but they can be heavy. Many years ago, the writers of "Europe on $5 a Day" advised people to tear out just the chapters they needed, but I hate to mutilate books (sort of like Mr. Bean and his Teddy.) I generally study several guide books before the trip and decide which one or two I will take. If others have supplementary information, I photocopy it to take along. When I've finished with a particular page, I can throw it away, or use the back for my own notes, which help me to recall the trip later. Put all your loose papers in a plastic bag or manila envelope.

A phrase book or pocket dictionary can be helpful, but you need to get acquainted with it before you actually need it. I spend most of my time on the food section, so I can order quickly, which is important in cafeterias. I often dine in small, out-of-the-way places where the servers do not speak English. Knowing how to pronounce the local words for various vegetables and meats leads to a pleasant dining experience.

Phrase books often have conversion tables between metric and the old "English" measurements. It's simpler to just start thinking in the new system, rather than converting all the time. A liter is just slightly more than a quart; why worry about 5 percent? A meter is a few inches longer than a yard, so you won't come home with a great deal of extra fabric. A kilogram is 2.2 pounds: 100 grams of cheese is a little under a quarter pound. Add some fruit and bread, have a picnic, and relax with the metric system.

Chapter Eight

UFOs:
UNCATEGORIZED
FLYING OBJECTS

Miscellany

A miniature flashlight can be good insurance, and costs little. One of the most common tourist injuries is a stubbed or broken toe from trying to walk in a dark, unfamiliar hotel room. I remember a Paris hotel in 1971, with the toilet down the hall at the end of a long, narrow room with the light switch near the door. The switch was on a timer, an all too short timer. Other travelers have had trouble trying to find the latrine located a quarter mile from their tent. Even in a luxury hotel, the power could go out, or there could be a fire. When you are in transit, it might be wise to remove the batteries, so they don't run down if the light is accidently switched on (less likely in a small plastic bag.)

A compass is a good tool for hiking, but some people also use one for urban touring. They say it helps them figure out where they are when they emerge from a subway station. Remember to find out what the declination is at your destination city.

There are ads for travel alarm clocks which are not much smaller than the regular wind-up type, and not cheap either. I've tried some miniature electronic clocks with mixed results. Then I realized that most men's wrist watches with alarms are pretty reliable, even the cheap ones. You just need manual dexterity. Don't wear an expensive watch; it's a magnet for thieves.

Any electrical appliances for travel should be lightweight and dual voltage, so you don't have to carry a converter (you still need adapter plugs for different outlet types.) These attributes do not add noticeably to the cost. I take a small electic shaver. If the weather is cool or your hairstyle demands it, you might want a hair dryer. As of this writing, you can buy a palm size 800 watt model from Franzus for $15. They also make a larger, 1500 watt model for $21, but why carry extra weight and bake out your hair even more quickly? Find out what voltage the hotel has before using appliances, and if it is even AC! I've heard of people burning out their hair dryers or curling irons with the wrong voltage. With cheap items, it might make sense to just buy them at your destination and give them away later. Even easier: Adopt a travel hairstyle which doesn't need them.

The travel iron or hair dryer can be helpful for drying your clothes if you are traveling in cool or damp weather. Otherwise, they may not be worth the weight.

SUNDRIES: Sometimes the Sun does not dry. If you intend to do any swimming or spend any time in a place without towels, you should have a "Body Chamois." This PVA material does for your skin what the old chamois skin did for your '57 Chevy. Rinse it, wring it, and it's ready to dry you. Wash it with mild detergent, and keep it in its plastic container, or a plastic bag. Small, cheap, and available at sporting goods stores.

Take facial tissues out of the box and put them in plastic bags. If toilet paper is needed where you are going, take a partial roll and flatten. We learned in the Girl Scouts to take sanitary supplies on every trip. Changes in activity, altitude or climate can change body rhythms just as jet lag changes body clocks. Be prepared.

Take only the manicure implements you intend to use, but include tweezers and small scissors. Add a mini sewing kit: A couple of needles and pins, thread wound around small cardboard (only the colors in your travel wardrobe) and extra shirt buttons and collar stays if appropriate. The small scissors might work for your mustache also. For longer trips, consider hair scissors (if you or a companion are used to cutting hair.) Barbers in some places might give you a shorter cut than you intended. Tape up some cardboard as a sheath for the blade end.

The metal objects, including needles and safety pins, go in a small checked box. Nail polish and remover can dissolve plastic bags. Wrap polish bottles securely in aluminum foil. Take the remover pads that come in handy foil packets.

If you wear shoes that require polishing, you may want a mini shoeshine kit. In many areas, getting a shoeshine on the street is putting yourself in a vulnerable position. If possible, wear low-luster shoes which can be cleaned with a damp tissue. Extra shoelaces are optional.

For picnics, you'll want can and bottle openers; not all bottles have twist-off caps. These, and the small knife must go in the checked box. A 12 cm (about 5") diameter plastic lid is compact, lightweight and makes an adequate cutting surface and plate for fruit or bakery items, outdoors or in your hotel room. If traveling by car, you can add more bulky equipment, such as electric hot pot and tea cups. Having a few of your favorite tea bags can be comforting on any trip. Your hotel should be able to provide a pot of hot water and cups. Many people find a small, dual voltage immersion heater to be convenient. You might also like to carry a tea bag in your day pack.

A magnesium fire starter and mosquito net are good for camping or remote areas. Most trips don't require them. If you expect to be "roughing it," check a camping department or sporting goods store for other survival items.

Chapter Nine

MAKING A LIST, CHECKING IT TWICE

The Complete Travel Checklists

Try not to be overwhelmed by the length of these check-lists. They are intended to cover a variety of travel situations, so you can choose which items to take on each trip. The first step, if you own this book, is to make a copy of each list for your own household use, but not for others. Copyright laws exist so authors can make a living from all their toil. Now there are a few ways that you can proceed. You can simply cross out those items you don't want to take on your trip. The remaining items can be checked off when you acquire them, and again when you pack them. If you are not sure about what to take, or you haven't yet had the chance to miniaturize everything possible, then you will need to prioritize the items as 1, 2 or 3. As you gradually acquire more tiny versions of gear, this process will become easier. If two or more people are traveling together, you can assign each sharable item to an individual, and put their initial next to it. Examples are guidebooks, picnic gear, electric items, detergent. You may be able to take everything on the lists this way.

BASIN KIT

_ _ Soap
_ _ Wash Cloth in Bag
_ _ Skin Buffer
_ _ Toothbrush
_ _ Toothpaste
_ _ Dental Floss
_ _ Plastic Cup
_ _ Plastic Safety Razor*
_ _ Anti-perspirant Stick
_ _ Skin Lotion
_ _ Sunscreen
_ _ Cotton Swabs
_ _ Make-up
_ _ Eye-pencil Sharpener*
_ _ Comb
_ _ Hair Pins and Clips*
_ _ Hair Dressing
_ _ Ear Plugs
_ _ Contact Lens Kit

* Items with an asterisk may not be allowed in a carry-on.
Put in small box to be checked, or purchase at destination.

SHOWER KIT

_ _   Soap or Body Wash
_ _   Shampoo
_ _   Conditioner
_ _   Dilution Bottle
_ _   Wide-tooth Comb
_ _   Hair Snare Drain Cover
_ _   Shower Cap
_ _   Spray Attachment
_ _   Hanging Clip

LAUNDRY KIT

_ _   Laundry Liquid
_ _   Stiff New Toothbrush
_ _   Vinyl Gloves
_ _   Universal Sink Plug
_ _   Plastic Hangers
_ _   Miniature Clothespins
_ _   Miniature Clothesline

DAY PACK

- _ _ Facial Tissues
- _ _ Handkerchief in Bag
- _ _ Mini Liquid Soap
- _ _ Mini Mirror
- _ _ Small Comb
- _ _ Lip Balm
- _ _ Lipstick or pencil
- _ _ Perfume Stick
- _ _ Pillbox
- _ _ Vitamins, etc.
- _ _ Lozenges
- _ _ Gum or Mints
- _ _ Adhesive Bandages
- _ _ Safety Pins*
- _ _ Emery Board
- _ _ Mosquito Repellant
- _ _ Sunscreen
- _ _ Sunglasses
- _ _ Indelible Ink Ballpoint
- _ _ Mini Notepad
- _ _ Mini Tape Measure
- _ _ Coin Purse or Two
- _ _ Small Amount of Cash
- _ _ Bottle Carrier
- _ _ Snack Food
- _ _ Small, Cheap Camera

PHARMACY KIT

_ _ Adhesive Bandages
_ _ Moleskin
_ _ Analgesic (pain relief)
_ _ Anti-diarrheal Medicine
_ _ Antihistamine
_ _ Birth Control
_ _ Cortisone Cream
_ _ Cough Drops
_ _ Decongestant
_ _ Echinacea
_ _ Ginger Capsules or other
_ _ Motion Sickness Prevent.
_ _ Goldenseal
_ _ Zinc Lozenges
_ _ Water Purifier
_ _ Your Prescriptions
_ _ Vitamins and Minerals
(list specifics here)

MONEY BELT

_ _ Passport
_ _ Driver's License
_ _ Travelers' Cheques
_ _ Cash
_ _ Credit Cards
_ _ Road Service Card
_ _ Telephone Call Card

PAPERWORK

_ _ Airline Tickets
_ _ Travel Passes
_ _ Copy of Passport Name Page
_ _ Visas and Extra Photos
_ _ Reservation Information
_ _ International Certificate of Vaccination
_ _ International Driver's License
_ _ International Student ID Card
_ _ Written Prescriptions
_ _ Credit Card Numbers
_ _ Travelers' Cheque Numbers
_ _ Frequent Flyer Numbers
_ _ Address Book or List
_ _ Writing Paper and Envelopes
_ _ Business Cards and Papers
_ _ Guidebooks and Maps
_ _ Phrase Book or Pocket Dictionary

MISCELLANY

- _ _ Spare Eyeglasses
- _ _ Facial Tissues
- _ _ Toilet Paper
- _ _ Sanitary Supplies
- _ _ Sewing Kit*
- _ _ Manicure Kit*
- _ _ Nail Polish
- _ _ Polish Remover Pads
- _ _ Hair Color
- _ _ Hair Scissors*
- _ _ Miniature Shoeshine Kit
- _ _ Spare Shoelaces
- _ _ Miniature Flashlight
- _ _ Alarm Watch or Clock
- _ _ Electric Shaver
- _ _ Hair Dryer
- _ _ Travel Iron
- _ _ Adaptor Plugs
- _ _ Voltage Converter
- _ _ Compass
- _ _ Body Chamois (small towel)
- _ _ Extra Plastic Bags
- _ _ Rubber Bands or Twist-ties
- _ _ Can and Bottle Openers*
- _ _ Small Knife*
- _ _ Spoon
- _ _ Plastic Lid as Plate

CLOTHING

_ _ Rubber Sandals
_ _ Swim Suit
_ _ Windbreaker
_ _ Crushable Hat
_ _ Shoes
_ _ Suit or
_ _ Slacks and Jacket
_ _ Extra Slacks or Skirt
_ _ Belt
_ _ Shirts
_ _ Tie
_ _ Cufflinks
_ _ Handkerchiefs
_ _ Underwear
_ _ Stockings
_ _ Lightweight Bathrobe
_ _ Pyjamas
_ _ Raincoat
_ _ Gloves
_ _ Scarves
_ _ Compact Umbrella

Chapter Ten

I SEE BY YOUR OUTFIT THAT YOU ARE A TOURIST

Creating Your Travel Wardrobe

Before you run out and buy a lot of clothing for your upcoming trip, consider whether you might not be better off if you built a wardrobe that would work for all your travels. This chapter will show you how to do that, and how to choose the particular items most appropriate to each destination and climate. Of course, if all you ever do is lie on a warm beach, you can get by with a swimsuit and sarong, but if you bought this book, it's a good bet your travels are more varied than that.

Some of these suggestions are geared toward men, and others are also appropriate for women, who should read this chapter before going on to the next one.

Do you travel for business, or occasionally dine at a three star restaurant? Then you need a suit or sportcoat, dress shirt and tie. Look for an easy-care fabric that won't wrinkle badly. This is one place you shouldn't turn up your nose at polyester, whether microfibre, regular, or in a blend. You should be able to hand wash the slacks, and remove spots on the coat without leaving a ring. I like navy, because it is readily available and is always proper. You can wear a navy suit to a coronation or dogfight. If you already have an easy-care outfit in another subdued color such as brown or dark olive, you can base your wardrobe on that.

Some people like to wear a nice wool suit for business. This is an option if your trip is short, or you have access to a speedy dry-cleaner. Remember that spills happen easily on airplanes. One woman was covered with food and beverages when an unsecured cart went flying down the aisle during turbulence.

If your travels do not require the coat, substitute a more casual jacket. At the very least, you should always take a lightweight nylon windbreaker, no matter where you are going. It takes very little space. Buy one with a hood that zips into the collar, and you may not need an umbrella. You still need the dark, easy-care slacks. You'll need a second pair of slacks while the first is being cleaned. If you anticipate warm weather, the second pair can be a lightweight cotton-poly blend in a lighter color, but choose something in the same color family, so all the shirts will go with both pairs. Do not take denim jeans. They are bulky and slow to dry. Even the blended fibre jeans are still not as compact as lightweight slacks.

Your selection of shirts is very important, both for comfort and appearance, so don't rush it. Ideally, you would like to blend in with the middle-class locals at your destination, instead of sticking out as a tourist. In some places, that means wearing a white shirt with dark slacks and shoes. You may choose not to be quite that strict, but you should not wear a tank top, or even a polo shirt, when visiting a big-city museum. I recommend some long-sleeve sport or dress shirts in subdued colors to go with the slacks. A subtle stripe or plaid may help to camouflage smudges and wrinkles. A cotton-poly blend will minimize wrinkles. For warm weather, look for at least 55% cotton. You might want a short-sleeve shirt for hot weather, but it won't protect your arms from the Sun. A light color long-sleeve shirt might be better. You can always roll up the sleeves a little. For cooler weather, consider a solid color turtleneck shirt. You can also layer it under a long-sleeve sport shirt for extra warmth. You should have four or five shirts total.

The heaviest wardrobe items are shoes, especially men's shoes. You may be able to get by with one pair if you buy comfortable walking shoes in black or brown leather. Do NOT wear brown shoes with navy or gray slacks. You will also need a pair of rubber sandals to wear at the pool or as slippers. In hot weather, you might prefer sandals as street wear, but this may not be a good idea if you want to visit a mosque, where you must remove your shoes, but keep your socks on. The sweaty and/or dusty feet of inconsiderate tourists are soiling the carpets where the local faithful must kneel down, bend over, and pray. So wear closed shoes and clean socks. Also, don't attempt to enter a mosque wearing shorts or a tank top. Covered legs and upper arms are in order. Actually, these are just good manners at any religious site.

You need a hat as protection from the Sun. Although some straw hats can be rolled up to fit in your bag, a cloth one will take up less space. Always take a swimsuit, even in Winter. Some hotels have an indoor pool or sauna. You'll want four sets of socks and underwear, as compact as possible. Bikini or low-rise shorts are a lot smaller than boxers. Although cotton is more comfortable, especially in hot weather, you should take at least one set of nylon, which may be the only set which dries overnight. Your robe should be lightweight silk or polyester, and not too long. If you must have pyjamas, the same applies. Don't forget handkerchiefs.

The wardrobe above should be fine for moderate temperatures and light rain showers. For colder and wetter conditions, add a nice raincoat in a color that goes with your dark slacks, a travel umbrella, and possibly gloves. A raincoat in a bright color screams "North American Tourist." If it's really cold, you might want a zip-out liner in your raincoat, but what will you do with it in warmer weather? It's pretty bulky to fit in your bag, and you don't want to carry it over your arm as you do the raincoat. Sweaters are bulky. I tried layering my windbreaker under my raincoat, and it worked about as well as a sweater. Your suit coat and a scarf could also give you that extra layer.

If you are visiting a hot climate and don't need to dress up for town, you could make both pairs of slacks a cotton-poly blend in light to medium colors, and throw in a pair of shorts. Add a T-shirt and you're ready for the fitness center. Make sure that all the shirts are light and cotton-rich. The basic wardrobe with dark suit would also be appropriate for a cruise, unless it's the type which requires a tuxedo (and formal shoes.) You don't want to cram all that into your carry-on bag. You could reserve the necessary items at a formal wear rental establishment in the port city, and fly there a day early to make sure you have everything at hand well before sailing. They have packages which include extra shirts and socks. Do not understate your waist measurement. In fact, add an inch, because most people grow appreciably on a cruise.

Putting together a travel wardrobe like this is a lot of work, especially getting all the colors to look well together. Some of the better department stores have personal shoppers to help you. You call them, tell them what you need, and make an appointment. They gather items in one place for your approval. If you don't like their selections, you are under no obligation to buy.

It's best to start with the coats, slacks, and shoes, and then add shirts as you find good matches. Don't let anyone talk you into combining two bright colors such as brick and royal. You should aim for a look of quiet elegance. Why? Imagine your flight is overbooked in coach class. Who has a better chance of being moved up to business or first class:

The guy wearing a tank top, or the gentleman with the nice shirt and perhaps a dark blazer? Who do you think is more likely to get free upgrades on rental cars or hotel rooms? These things don't happen all the time, but a neat appearance improves your odds. You are also more likely to get invited to people's homes during your travels if you dress conservatively.

Some people like to wear a sweatsuit on the plane for comfort. This is a bulky and unnecessary wardrobe item. Better to wear slacks with some elastic in the waist, or buy them one inch larger and wear a belt. Women sewing zippered slacks might like to modify the pattern pieces as follows: Add one half inch at the waist to the side seams of the front and back. Add two inches to the waistband length. Choose some elastic the width of desired finished waistband, 1" to 1.5" (2.5 cm to 4 cm). To figure the length, subtract two inches from YOUR waist measurement, and add the amount the waistband overlaps at the ends. After attaching the waistband to the outside of the slacks and sewing the end seams, sew the elastic securely to the ends, and then slipstitch the inside of the waistband. With this method, the elastic replaces the interfacing.

If you lay all the wardrobe items out on your bed, you can get a good idea of how the pieces work together. If it seems like too much to fit in the bag, remember that you will be wearing one complete outfit, including the bulkiest items of shoes and coat. If you must take extra shoes, you can put miscellaneous items such as electric shaver in them.

Men's wardrobe

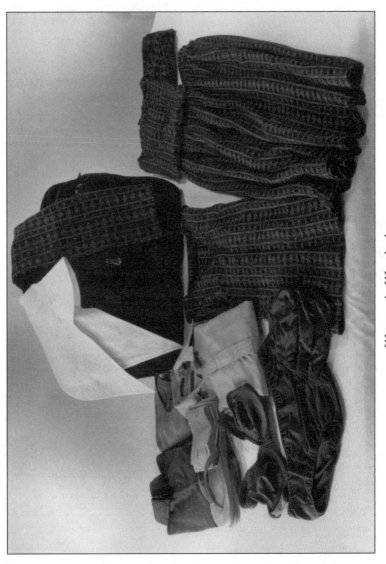

Chapter Eleven

I ENJOY BEING A GIRL

Wardrobe Modifications for Women

Women can follow the wardrobe planning suggestions in the previous chapter, but they also have other options and advantages. Their suit jackets need not be quite as "constructed" as men's, and their clothing tends to be smaller and lighter weight. This means they can probably add an item or two to the basic list. They can also get away with wearing brighter colors, and have more design options. Some women prefer slacks, others skirts. If you take both, you can handle most situations. However, short skirts are not acceptable in many places. I recommend mid-calf length as the best compromise between modesty and utility. As a side benefit, you can use knee-high stockings instead of pantyhose. They take less space, are easier to wash and dry, and a run only ruins half the pair. A fancy blouse and a long skirt which matches the suit jacket will handle formal occasions. Ultrasuede is good here.

Many women believe they have to take a "dress" and there are even ads for the "indispensible travel dress" which is just a dark dress made of nylon and lycra so it won't wrinkle. You probably won't be comfortable wearing it in warm weather. Worse, you won't be able to access your moneybelt without lifting the dress to your waist, a serious problem in public places. A better idea is a two piece "dress" of matching separates. You can wash the top or bottom separately, and use them with other items in your travel wardrobe. Make your clothes work hard for you.

If you are going to spend more than a few days in a place where all the local women wear long skirts and/or head scarves, you might consider following their example, in order to attract less attention. At the very least, avoid shorts and short skirts. Wearing any style of head scarf is better than none; styles vary by region anyway. You'll also protect your hair from the Sun, and save styling time.

Following are some sample wardrobes for different situations. Once you have acquired the basic pieces, feel free to substitute or hybridize. For moderately cool weather, daytime temperature 10 to 23 degrees Celsius or 50 to 74 degrees Fahrenheit, some rain likely: Dark raincoat with hood or matching hat and shoes. Two pairs of slacks, same color as coat. Four shirts: One white or pastel long-sleeve, one stripe or print long-sleeve, one print short-sleeve, one solid long-sleeve turtleneck. For business, substitute a three-piece suit of jacket, slacks and skirt for the two pairs of slacks. For dressy occasions, add a two-piece dress in a print that can be used with the solid color pieces.

For slightly warmer weather, daytime temperature 15 to 28 degrees Celsius or 59 to 82 degrees Fahrenheit, and not much rain: A pair of dark slacks with jacket or nylon windbreaker in same color. Add a four-piece ensemble of lightweight, breathable, drapey fabric such as rayon in a low-key print that coordinates with the dark slacks. The four pieces are long pants, mid-calf skirt, sleeveless or short-sleeve blouse, and tunic-length overblouse. The pieces should be just roomy enough to allow air circulation and the skirt just wide enough at the hem to allow a comfortable stride. Add a long sleeve light color shirt and a couple of neat looking cotton knit tops. If you sew the ensemble yourself, or have it made, buy extra fabric for a long scarf, which can be worn on your head, neck, shoulders, or waist for different looks. An ensemble like this is not difficult to sew if you choose pull-on pants and skirt (elastic waist, no zipper) and is comfortable on long flights.

For weather that is guaranteed to be warm, even hot, daytime temperature 20 to 35 degrees Celsius, or 68 to 95 degrees Fahrenheit, rain highly unlikely: An unlined cotton or blend jacket with a matching or coordinating brimmed hat. A kimono style jacket will allow air circulation, and a print will help to camouflage wrinkles. Slacks and/or skirts in lightweight, breathable fabrics, in solid colors to go with the jacket. A long-sleeve, breathable pastel shirt, and a few short-sleeve or sleeveless shirts. Tee shirts that fit properly look much neater than those which are too tight, too loose, or have dropped shoulder seams. What about tank tops? Well, some are cute, and some look trashy. Unfortunately, some of the cutest ones have very narrow straps, exposing your bra straps. You can minimize the sloppy appearance if your bra is exactly the same color as the top. Otherwise, forget it. Also forget it if you are larger than average. And, for anyone wearing a tank top, keep that jacket with you in case of religious sites or air conditioning.

Another item you will want to have is a visored scarf, for which I've given you a pattern in this book. Choose a lightweight cotton-poly blend in a light to medium color. 3/4 yard (70 cm) is enough to make two. The brim has medium to stiff interfacing between two layers of finish fabric. Seams are 1/2" or 12 mm, and edges are 1/4" or 6 mm, folded twice. An easy project.

Of course, you will always include some type of windbreaker (or the cotton or blend jacket mentioned above.) Other essential items are the rubber sandals and swimsuit. You might be able to find a very compact swimsuit in the lingerie department, and for very little money. I found a bra that had no visible hardware, just a hidden clasp in front. The material was stretchy and required no strap adjustments. I could have bought a matching bikini, but it was cut high on the leg, and I hate swimsuits that ride up, so I made a hip-hugger bottom in the same color stretch fabric. Make sure you choose a dark color; the lighter ones become transparent when wet. If you think this option too revealing, I must tell you it afforded a lot more coverage than a bikini I bought in Rome. But the lingerie option is not recommended for those whose bras are designed by bridge builders. The swimsuit should be a quick-dry fabric with no padding.

You'll want four pairs of panties, one or two bras, and perhaps six pairs (all the same color) of knee-high stockings, so that you will still have four pairs at the end of the trip. Nylon can be blotted half-dry with a towel, and will dry quickly. There are other fibre inventions that purport to have a more "cottony" feel, but they are very expensive, and sometimes have wider elastic, which adds bulk and drying time. For the fitness center, the most compact and quick drying item is a nylon leotard. For cold weather, add tights, which can also be worn under other clothes.

If you need a robe, flimsy is what you want, but here's another creative alternative: A "cover-up" shirt long enough to cover your bottom. Some men's dress shirts have long enough tails. Wear it in the evening in your hotel room, and during the day for Sun protection. Men's sleeves are also about two inches longer, so you can unbutton the cuffs and let them help cover your hands on long hikes. Turn up the collar for neck protection. So if

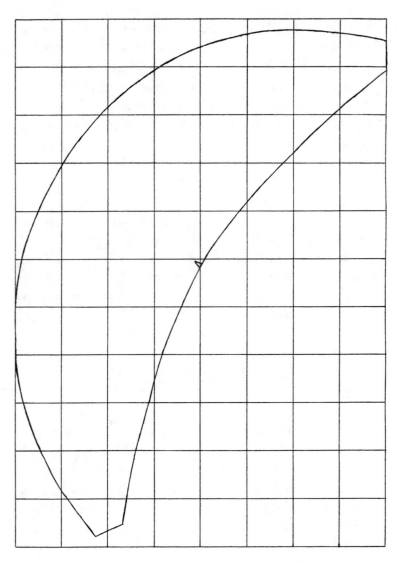

make lines 1″ = 2.54 cm apart

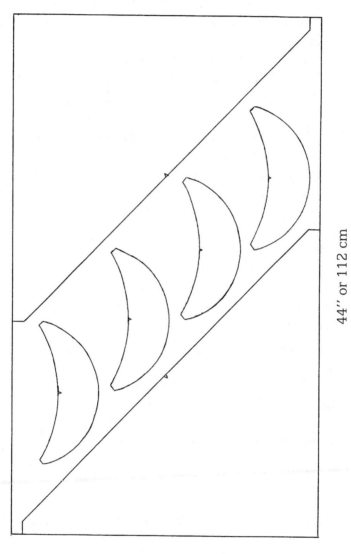

27" or 69 cm

44" or 112 cm

you were planning to buy a long-sleeve cotton blend shirt, consider the men's department; it will most likely be cheaper too. Depending on the maker and cut, a men's small (neck 14 and 1/2) will probably fit up to a 37" chest. The hip measurements may be smaller on men's shirts. If in doubt, try them on, or bring a tape measure.

For a cruise vacation, even a formal one, you don't have to take more than one bag. Take a long, dark skirt that is not bulky. Choose an A-line skirt just wide enough at the hem for dancing, in a poly-cotton blend with a slight sheen, or a dark, pleated polyester chiffon. Work that skirt! Add a couple of compact tops. Some suggestions: A black skirt with a black lace top, plus a sapphire or other jewel-tone chiffon top. A brown skirt would look great with gold tissue lamé. Avoid heavily beaded or fussy fabrics. For shoes, your basic dark pumps are more practical for dancing than sandals. Add some decorative clips if you like, and be glad you don't have to deal with a tuxedo, etc. For non-dressy vacations, I often get by with just one pair of shoes: Leather moccasins with cushion soles.

It is much more important that your outfits be appropriate, comfortable, and easily washable, than that they be numerous. The point of most vacations is to SEE, not to BE SEEN, and while classy-looking clothes may get you better treatment, flashy clothes may attract the kind of attention you don't want.

I Enjoy Being A Girl

Dressy Business Suit

Casual Suit with Scarf

Chapter Twelve

GOING IN STYLE

Color Coordination
and Design Considerations

Achieving a "together" appearance requires some rudimentary knowledge about "what goes with what." Color is one of the most important factors. Certainly you want every top to go with every bottom in your travel wardrobe, and the safest way to do this is by staying within the same color family. On a very basic level, you can separate colors into cool, i.e., blue and purple, or warm, i.e., orange and yellow, categories. However, within each simple color are sub-colors which are warmer or cooler than their brethren. For example, within what we commonly call red, fuschia is more cool than tomato. Within yellow, school-bus is warmer than lemon. Thick books have been written on color theory, and I'm not going to duplicate them here. What I'll give you is a list of colors which are compatible with the readily available basic colors.

The best thing you can do at the outset is to visit a fabric or department store with a color-savvy friend, and drape stuff around your neck to find out which groups of colors look nice with your skin, hair and eyes. There are color "systems" which purport to tell you to which "season" or "color-key" you belong, but these are simplistic. You are unique, and there is no substitute for experimentation. Once you know which colors make your skin glow or your eyes sparkle, your life will be forever changed.

COLOR COMBINATIONS FOR MEN

Navy:	White, Pale Lavender-Blue, Pale Blue, French Blue, Royal, Light Grey.
Black:	Same as Navy, plus Grey, Stone, Aqua, Teal.
Grey:	Same as Black.
Forest:	White, Cream, Pale Green, Pale Blue, Pale Lavender, Aqua, Sage, Stone, Light Grey, Tan.
Dark Olive:	White, Pale Lavender, Pale Blue, Pale Yellow, Warm Beige, Khaki.
Brown:	Cream, Pale Yellow, Pale Apricot, Warm Beige, Khaki, Tan, Rust.

If you want to add more zip to your outfits, you can use small quantities of brighter colors from the women's list below in your ties or in a subtle stripe in your shirt.

COLOR COMBINATIONS FOR WOMEN

Navy:	Add Periwinkle, True Red and Kelly Green to Men's List.
Black or Grey:	Add any bright color that looks good.
Forest:	Add Deeper Lavender and Turquoise-Green.
Dark Olive:	Add Pink, Rose and small amounts of Fuschia.
Brown:	Add Peach and Metallic Gold.

THE PROBLEM WITH PASTELS

White slacks and shoes are appropriate in hot weather, but keeping them looking fresh can be a problem. Even if you are careful, you will eventually acquire a smudge line at the hem, and scuff marks on the shoes. If you decide to bleach the slacks, wear protective gloves (and very little else, because splatters will ruin other colors.) The tub is the safest place. Leave the remaining bleach for the cleaning staff. Do not attempt to carry it in your bag; the only thing worse would be explosives. At least you can bleach white cotton; this is not an option with pastels. For white leather shoes, clean with soap, then try a white nail pencil. If this doesn't work, take them to a shoe repair shop for polishing.

AVOIDING FASHION FAUX-PAS

You probably already know not to wear flesh color slacks, or a floral tie with a plaid shirt, but some mistakes are more subtle. Sweatpants and sweatshirt are not figure flattering, and are much too bulky. You shouldn't have too many things going on in your outfit. Do not mix two different prints. Even a two-tone windbreaker can mess you up, limiting your choice of shirts. A plaid shirt might be fine with a plain coat, but over-the-top with a tweed one. A shirt that is slightly lighter than the slacks usually looks better than the other way around, but a darker blazer is OK.

If your skirt is a print with dark colors, it is better to choose one of those colors for a shirt, instead of white, which would add another layer of contrast. With a solid color skirt, white would be OK. A jacket with diagonal seaming is not the one to wear with a paisley skirt: Too much difference in the shapes and motives. Remember the KISS principle: Keep It Simple....

Chapter Thirteen

NEW THREADS

Fibres and Fabrics

The following list of fibres and their attributes will help you make informed decisions about your travel clothing based on anticipated climate and other factors. Often the behavior of the fibre will depend on how it is woven or knitted.

WOOL: Often admired for its appearance and warmth, wool is not practical for most travel. The wovens usually require dry-cleaning, and the knits are slow to dry. Unless it's a short trip or you have a speedy, reliable dry-cleaner nearby, leave it at home.

LINEN: Guaranteed to wrinkle terribly. The blends which resist wrinkles are mostly polyester and rayon with only a token amount of linen.

COTTON: More comfortable than synthetic fibres in humid weather, but slower to dry, and more wrinkle-prone. Lightweight knit shirts are good. For wovens, a blend with polyester will cut down on wrinkles.

RAMIE: Generally used in blends to add lustre.

RAYON (and other processed cellulose): Cottony or silky depending on filament and weave. Drapey and comfortable. Wrinkles can be removed more easily, at lower temperature than cotton. A blend with polyester will wrinkle less.

SILK: Very compact and lightweight. The knits are excellent for shirts and long underwear. Washable wovens are a good choice for a bathrobe if you don't care about wrinkles.

POLYESTER: This synthetic fibre shows up in many forms. The old double-knit was the butt of many jokes, but it did not wrinkle and it was easy to clean. The silky polyester shirts are clammy in humid weather, but the cotton blends are a traveler's best friend. Just remember that they won't release oils and perspiration odors as easily as 100% cotton, and they tend to pill, so launder with care. Microfibres shed water and are lightweight, making them an excellent choice for raincoats, and even blazers, if you don't mind the high-tech sheen. Some of the mesh weaves and knits are conducive to air and moisture transfer.

NYLON: Inexpensive and compact choice for underwear and socks. Dries quickly. Spandex blends are good for swimsuits, leotards and tights. There is also a heavier, tougher, more cottony feeling nylon used for active wear.

ACRYLIC: All the bulk of wool without all the warmth. Awkward to hand wash and hang dry.

HIGH-TECH FLEECE: A better choice for cold weather, as it is easy to wash and dry, and provides good insulation.

GORE-TEX®: Fabric laminated to a membrane with tiny holes which keep water droplets out, but allow perspiration vapor to escape. Excellent for heavy rain and ski wear. Expensive.

ULTRASUEDE®: A synthetic material with the look of suede. Washable and wrinkle-resistant, and therefore a good alternative to wool, in the same climate range. Expensive.

If unsure about a fabric's wrinkle resistance, squeeze a wad of it in your hot little hand: The hotter, the better. After a few seconds of this, if you don't like the look of it, don't buy it. This is standard operating procedure in fabric stores. If the people in Neiman-Marcus don't like it, tough! You want clothing that performs well, and they have steamers for the wrinkles.

Cotton, Rayon and Silk usually shrink the first time they are washed. If you are sewing garments, simply wash and iron the fabric before you cut out the pieces. If buying a garment, check all the tags to see if the manufacturer pre-washed, or if there is an estimate on expected shrinkage. Without such information, you should plan for the possibility that the garment may shrink 1"-2" in both length and width.

Warm Weather Jacket

Chapter Fourteen

SOME LIKE IT HOT, SOME LIKE IT COLD

Clothing for Extreme Conditions

Previous chapters contained wardrobe suggestions for the moderate weather you are likely to encounter on your vacation, but what do you wear if you are called to Helsinki or Stockholm in December? Black stretch ski pants are warmer than regular slacks and easier to tuck into boots. Look for a blended fabric that is washable. For extra warmth, add black silk underwear or nylon tights. Ski pants can look elegant with a dressy parka or coat. Don't forget a matching hat or hood, and some warm gloves. For dressy occasions, here's a tip from some women in Alaska: Wear a long skirt to cover your long underwear.

If you anticipate very heavy rain, a Gore-tex® raincoat, or even a rainsuit, will be your best protection. There are even Gore-tex® hiking boots, since it's even more important to keep your feet dry. These are all expensive items, but if you were thinking of buying a new ski suit anyway, it might make sense to buy one that could also be used for rain. Pick one of the more sub-dued colors or you'll look like a highway worker.

It's more likely that you have planned your trip for moderate weather, with a lightweight raincoat such as microfibre, but no boots, because they are bulky. If the urban puddles get too deep, try to find some inexpensive rubber boots or shoe covers that you can either give away later, or put in your bag, or put in a box to check.

Most people plan their vacations to avoid cold or rainy weather, and so they are likely to encounter hot weather. I can't fathom why anyone would freely choose to go to Athens (either Georgia or Greece) in the Summer, when the temperature is likely to hit 35 to 40 degrees Celsius (95 to 104 degrees Fahrenheit) but every year, tens of thousands of people do it, and most of them live to tell about it. If you want to be among the survivors, you need to be careful. Visit the outdoor sites in the morning when they open. Spend the afternoon in the air-conditioned museum, or at least in the shade with a cool drink. Carry your water bottle with you at all times. Sleeveless shirts are OK if you are in the shade, but if you are going to be in the Sun for more than 15 minutes during the day, you should wear a long-sleeve, light color shirt, and a brimmed scarf or hat. Fabrics should be very breathable, even at the cost of wrinkles.

In many places, the locals will rest after lunch and emerge again in the evening. If your hotel is nearby, you might do the same. You could do a little laundry, soak your feet in cold water, plan tomorrow's excursions, or take a nap. You'll be in better shape to enjoy your dinner, and maybe go dancing afterward.

Ready for Sun

Ready for Rain

Chapter Fifteen

THE WRONG STUFF

Things You Should Not Take

There are items which should not be taken on board an aircraft, neither in your carry-on nor in checked luggage. Some of these are obviously hazardous, others less so. You shouldn't take anything explosive or flammable. That includes large quantities (over one pint) of flammable perfume, as well as any amount of fireworks, butane lighters, or strike-anywhere matches. Regular matches may only be carried on your person, presumably on the theory that, if they ignite, you will be the first to know.

A better alternative for backwoods survival is the small block of magnesium available in sporting goods stores. Magnesium is a lightweight element which is very fire resistant in a thick piece, but explosive in small particles. With a knife, you scrape off a small pile of shavings, and get your tinder ready. On the other side of the block, you scrape the striker with the back of the knife to create the spark you need to ignite the shavings and tinder. Undisturbed, the little block should behave itself.

You shouldn't take any type of compressed gas, including aerosol cans, SCUBA tanks, carbon dioxide cartridges and self-inflating rafts. Do not take anything corrosive, such as drain cleaners, solvents or strong acids. That includes wet cell batteries. Nail polish remover in a bottle is a disaster waiting to happen in your luggage anyway; take the foil lined packages of remover pads instead. Do not take anything that is infectious, poisonous or radioactive. Exceptions would be small amounts of medicines or toiletries.

Do not take pepper spray or tear gas. If you need to transport firearms and/or ammunition, they must be in safe containers in checked luggage, not in your carry-on, and you must alert the airline personnel to their existence. If you try to transport hazardous substances, U.S. law provides for criminal penalties up to $500,000 and five years. Your safety is also at stake.

Then there are the items that you are not allowed to bring into certain countries. Agricultural areas don't allow vegetables, fruit or meat which could contain an infectious pest that might threaten their crops. You can't blame them. California has had very bad experiences with the Mediterranean fruit fly and other pests. In some countries, alcoholic beverages are not allowed, usually because of Islamic or other regulations. A friend of mine spent a few hours in a Saudi Arabian airport, trying to explain to the officials that ginger ale is a soft drink and not an alcoholic beverage. He didn't convince them.

You can't have chewing gum in certain countries, because some inconsiderate slobs threw theirs on the sidewalk, and ruined the situation for everyone. Actually, you can chew it in your hotel, but not out in public, and you need to smuggle it in.

Some countries require women to wear long skirts, not slacks, and some places prohibit shorts for everyone, so it's best to check ahead. There are places where the only footwear available or affordable by the locals are rubber thong sandals. If you wear expensive Teva type sandals, you will stand out, and someone may covet them enough to steal them, along with the shirt off your back.

Although U.S. dollars are accepted (sometimes preferred) in many places, in some countries it is illegal to use them. Check with the relevant Government Tourist Office or Embassy ahead of time to find out what items are prohibited.

Firms which do business with government agencies, especially defense contractors, often tell employees not to carry obvious identification of their employment. Government officials and high level executives might do the same. It is usually safest to travel as an ordinary tourist.

Don't wear an expensive watch or jewelry on any of your travels; they are prime targets for muggers everywhere. Put them in your safe deposit box before you leave. Some people advise women who are traveling solo to wear a wedding ring to discourage unwanted advances. This may or may not be effective, depending on the circumstances, but I wouldn't wear an expensive, solid gold ring.

You don't want your house keys lost or stolen on a trip. Besides the inconvenience, you'd worry about a stranger entering your house. It is better to leave them with a trusted neighbor, most logically the one who is watering your houseplants. You could also hide one key somewhere on your property, but not within ten feet of the door, or under a rock, or some other obvious place. Before one trip, we forgot to take the last two pieces of fruit from the bowl, and had to ask our neighbor to get rid of them before they rotted and attracted insects.

Now that sharp metal objects are no longer allowed in carry-on luggage, people are wondering what to do about grooming aids such as scissors, clippers and sewing needles. Even tweezers are being confiscated! Some people are buying these items at their destination, but it can get expensive if one flies frequently. Buying all the asterisk marked items on the lists could easily run $20, and also requires some time investment. An alternative: Put those items in a small, corrugated cardboard box labeled with your name and destination address, and check it at the airport. If it doesn't arrive on your flight, immediately apply to the airline to reimburse you for first night necessities. If it doesn't arrive at your hotel later (and overseas there may not be delivery service) you can buy what you need, but now you'll be using the airline's money. Don't carry the box for the whole trip; just scrounge a new one before each flight.

Chapter Sixteen

THE GOOD, THE BAD, AND THE UGLY

Great Idea or Gimmick?

There are hundreds of products that promise to make your travel easier, but you should examine them with a skeptical eye before plunking down your hard-earned cash. Different circumstances demand different solutions of course, but sometimes the solution to a problem only changes the problem, and sometimes it is just plain laughable. I hope to save you some real money here.

There are bags with a zippered gusset which allows them to expand, presumably to accomodate all the goods you acquire during your trip. This may seem like a stupid question, but if the bag fit under the seat before, and now must be thrown in the hold, how is this an improvement? Expandable bags are necessarily soft, and vulnerable to damage. See the Shipping chapter for better ideas.

Yes, I've carried home a bottle of Kirschwasser from Germany, and Tequila from Mexico, and they did cost less than at home, but it usually isn't worth babysitting glass bottles just to save a small amount of money.

There are hanging toiletries kits which roll or fold for packing, and these can be very handy if you have a place to hang them in the bathroom, such as the shower rod or robe hook. You can also buy inexpensive hanging clips and clip them to your clear plastic toiletries bag. Zippered freezer bags will slip out of the clips; you need a bag with a heavier zipper to hold. Many people use both hanging and stand-up kits; choose the ones that work best for your gear and travel style.

If you take a curling iron, you will find the insulated carrier (similar to an oven mitt) to be useful; you can pack the iron while it is still warm. There are now mesh and/or vinyl organizing bags and folders for clothing, but they aren't cheap, and each bag is equivalent to adding another shirt to your pile! For small and easily snagged items such as stockings, the plastic sandwich or freezer bags work better, and weigh practically nothing.

Travel stores are convenient places to pick up many of the items you need, but they'll also tempt you with items you don't. As with most shopping, it is best to go with a list. Other places where you might find the listed items are drug, department, sporting goods and craft stores. I went backpacking in the Girl Scouts, and always volunteered for the food detail in order to make sure I ate well. Way back then, there weren't a lot of freeze-dried foods, and we could not have afforded to buy them anyway. We found a sufficient variety of lightweight, non-perishable foods in the supermarket. Gold is wherever you find it.

Reversible dresses, skirts, and blouses are really not helpful. They are nearly twice as heavy and bulky as having two different items, the only difference being the facings. You have to wash them just as often to remove perspiration, and they take longer to dry. As for reversible coats, if you planned your wardrobe correctly, you don't need two colors.

Women who want to add more variety to their business suit without taking more than four blouses might try the following: One of the blouses should have short sleeves and a scoop neck. Over it, you can wear fancy scarves or dickeys. Several of these will pack in the space of one shirt. To keep a scarf in place, attach small safety pins to the inside of the jacket on each side of the top button and slip scarf ends through them. Underarm dress shields, either washable or disposable, could reduce shirt laundry.

Pants with zip-off legs are OK for hiking in the mountains; in urban areas, they look too casual. Jackets with zip-off sleeves: If it's that hot, do you still need a vest? And where will you stow the sleeves? It depends on your particular circumstance: Are you mountain trekking or urban touring? After decades of experience with both, I find that a windbreaker and a variety of shirts will handle most situations with minimum bulk. Insulated jackets are for cold weather; unzip the front if you need to, but don't remove the sleeves!

Some people have a system for lightening the load gradually, and avoiding laundry. They take old clothes, wear them until they are dirty, and then give them away. This would only work for a fairly short trip where you don't care if you look like a hobo. This tip was included for chuckles. In most cases, you want to take a small amount of nice looking clothing which is easy to wash.

Other people use their raincoat as a bathrobe. I prefer the long dress shirt, which is also comfortable for reading in bed, but you can buy robes which fold up into practically nothing anyway. I think pyjamas waste space, but if you need them against the cold, silk underwear is most compact, and serves two purposes.

Someone has marketed a line of travel separates for women that are very compact and wrinkle-resistant. They are a nylon-spandex blend, like leotard material. If you don't mind looking as if you just came from ballet practice, and the weather isn't too warm or humid, they are OK, but certainly not the best all-around choice. Your travel wardrobe should consist of clothing you wouldn't feel silly wearing out to dinner in your home town.

Chapter Seventeen

PACKING IT IN

The Art of Arrangement

An earlier chapter advised packing all the small items in clear plastic bags so you can find them easily. In general, you'll want to put the heavier items on the bottom, and your clothes on top, except for items you may need in transit. You'll probably refine your packing system to take advantage of any compartments your luggage may have. For example, if there is a large, flat section, you might use it for your paperwork. Small, zippered, outer compartments are good for items you want to find in a hurry and which might otherwise sink to the bottom of the main section.

There seem to be as many different methods of packing clothes as there are travelers, and they usually involve trade-offs. Here are some of them; pick your poison.

To minimize wrinkles, some people fold each item around tissue paper or the lightweight plastic bags used by dry-cleaners. Others stack clothing on the bed and fold all the items together as a unit, so the "innies" act as tissue paper for the "outies." Some put socks, undies and tee shirts in a core bag and fold the outer clothes around them. These methods work best with the suitcases which open up completely to give you a large flat area. There will be more fold lines with the "top-loading" bags. Bundle methods assume that you hang up all items each night and that you don't have to unwrap en route. This is now a serious drawback with the extremely thorough airport inspections. Also, as the temperature drops on the airplane or late in the day, you may want to reach in the bag for a long sleeve shirt or extra layer.

If your bag has a thin, flat compartment, you can use it for your paperwork and a dress shirt. You can even use the envelope in place of the original cardboard your shirt was wrapped around. Fabrics which do not wrinkle badly can be rolled up, which allows for easy retrieval. I just fold my clothes carefully and live with the wrinkles. No matter what system you use, there will always be some fold lines. At the very least, you have to fold in the sleeves. Items with gathers, pleats, darts or curved seams are susceptible to wrinkles under any system. The best solution is wrinkle-resistant fabric, or using a hotel iron.

If you carry extra shoes, you must put them in bags to avoid dirt transfer. I prefer clear plastic bags to the cloth shoe covers because they are easy to wipe clean, and cheap to replace. They are also good for rubber sandals which are still damp. To save space, you can put some miscellaneous items inside the shoes.

Small items can go in a side pocket or a plastic bag. I like to put the nylon windbreaker at the top of the main compartment for quick retrieval. This is especially helpful if you land in foggy San Francisco on a June evening. In transit, it helps to have the basin kit within easy reach. I like to take the opportunity to wash my face and brush my teeth at airport stopovers. It is best not to use the airplane washroom for these things; other people are standing in line with more pressing needs. Some women like to completely redo their make-up in the washroom before they land; this is one of the most inconsiderate things to do.

If you take a spare pair of eyeglasses, put them in a hard case and/or pack them in the middle of the bag. The same applies for other breakable items, just in case someone handles your bag who is not as gentle with it as you. I can't remember having anything break in a carry-on, but can't say the same for checked luggage.

If you are bringing home gifts, you may be able to nest them: I was able to fold four meters of lightweight fabric to fit inside a moderate size handbag in place of the original packing paper. I managed to fold a sweater into another handbag. Be creative, but don't seal packages.

If a friend or relative asks you to bring back something fragile, such as glassware or pottery, either decline, or ask them if they are willing to pay for the store to send it to them, insured. Otherwise, the broken item will make everyone feel badly. People who don't travel widely think you can carry anything!

It's in the Bag with room to spare, weight under 8 kg

Chapter Eighteen

YOU SEND ME

Shipping Packages

If your trip requires a lot of bulky or heavy equipment, and you don't want to schlep it to the airport, you can send it to your destination ahead of time via the Postal Service, UPS, etc. Make sure the folks at your destination, either relatives, or hotel keepers, know to expect it. This works well within North America, but overseas air can get expensive.

If, near the end of your overseas trip, you see that you have collected more stuff in the trunk of your rental car than could possibly fit in your bag, you have options. Surface mail is good for items such as books and tourist brochures which are not fragile, not subject to duty, and would add significant weight or bulk to your bag. (Your other duty-free allowance applies only to items that accompany you.) Use your indelible ink pen to label and address all packages. Allow the post office to inspect all parcels before sealing them. In low wage countries, virgin stamps are a temptation: Have them cancelled in your sight. Other candidates for lower cost surface mail: Unbreakable, low duty items you won't need for a few months.

You can pay exhorbitant rates for airmail, or you can be your own air courier. Get an inexpensive hard suitcase or even a sturdy corrugated box which can easily be opened for inspection. Put the least valuable items in it to be checked. This may mean you put some of your clothes in there, and put the expensive or fragile items in your carry-on.

Reputable stores are pretty good at packing fragile items and shipping them to you or a friend. If you really get carried away with shopping, you can go to a worldwide freight company, where, for a flat fee, they give you a large box to fill, and then send it by air. This is an expensive option, but worth knowing about. You'll have less worry if you buy items that are small and not too fragile, such as jewelry, paperweights, scarves, and small leather goods. Lightweight clothing is an option. For the seamstress on your list, several meters of silk fabric take up surprisingly little space.

For travel within the U.S., consider having expensive out-of-state purchases shipped home to avoid a large state sales tax. This may not work with overseas purchases. Your local post office collects the duty and may alert the state tax collector. For current information on customs, get the free pamphlet "Know Before You Go" from the U.S. Customs Service (see Sources chapter) or any passport agency.

In Canada, the national Goods and Services Tax, or GST, can be refunded to you at the airport or border or by mail, with a $50 Canadian minimum per saved receipt. You must fill out the refund form at the store or hotel.

In Europe, the Value Added Tax, or VAT, is high, the minimum purchase qualifying for a refund is high, and it varies by country. You send the paperwork back to the store and then wait for your refund. We did it with a Burberry's raincoat, and it worked. Some stores have now joined a consortium, ETS (evade taxes sooner?), to give you the refund when you leave the country. Look for their logo and look forward to their 20% commission.

You may be able to save thousands of dollars in sales tax on a new car. For California, if you take delivery of an auto elsewhere, and have it with you for more than 90 days before you bring it into California, you do not have to pay the use tax (same rate as the sales tax) which would otherwise be due upon registration. You will need documentation to prove that the car was actually in your possession outside the state for more than 90 days. In addition to saving the tax, you save the expense of car rental. So if you are planning a long trip, and thinking about buying a foreign car, this may be a good opportunity. Your local dealer can arrange the purchase of a car which meets your state's requirements, to be picked up at the factory, and shipped home after you've driven it abroad.

Chapter Nineteen

TWO MONTHS
FOR THE PRICE OF ONE

Money Saving Tips

If you believe the monetary values assigned to the trip prizes on TV game shows, a one week trip for two costs $5,000 to $10,000, and only the wealthy can afford a vacation. The truth is that you can travel comfortably for far less than these inflated prices. There are vacation possibilities in every price range.

Lodging is a major expense on most trips. People on a very tight budget can use campgrounds and hostels. Here are some ideas for saving money in the moderate category. If you are traveling to a different town each day, you can stay at inexpensive places for three nights, and then stay one night at a hotel with lots of amenities. This is the place to do laundry, wash your hair, and relax. If you spend $40 three times plus $120 once, your average is $60 per night, and you have the benefits of the better hotel often enough to restore your cleanliness and spirit. In some countries, the price spread could be $8 to $160.

In many hotels, you can negotiate a discount, but don't try it in the place charging only $8! In more expensive places, give the desk clerk an excuse for a discount: You plan to stay at least three nights, you're a senior citizen or member of a travel club, or you're traveling on business and want the corporate rate. Unless the hotel expects to be full, you can usually get a discount of at least 10%. This is another reason for traveling with just one bag; it is easy to head for another hotel down the street. Often, the desk clerk will relent and call you back. Some hotels do not like to discount, but may offer you a deluxe room or suite for the price of a standard room. If you expect to spend a lot of time in your room, this can be worthwhile. Conversely, you can sometimes negotiate a good deal by taking an attic room or one without a view. Sometimes you can size up the room situation by what the desk clerk tells the people ahead of you.

I don't usually reserve hotel rooms in advance, because I don't know exactly where I will be each night. However, I do reserve a hotel room for the first night after a long flight. The easiest way is to call the toll-free number of a hotel chain which has a property in the destination city. If you know when you will arrive in a particular city, ask for suggestions. Sometimes a resident of one city will know a hotel keeper in another, and even make the call on your behalf. This networking can benefit everyone concerned.

Airfare is another major expense. You can save a lot of

money by planning ahead and being flexible. Figure out in advance how early you'd be willing to fly out, how late you can return, and how few or many days you can stay. Also figure out which airports you are willing to use. Call the airlines late at night, when the agents have more time to help you. Tell them that you are shopping for a low fare, and how flexible you are. If you have never done this before, you will be amazed at the difference in fares on the same routes. I've gotten some great deals by planning ahead. One time I saved a bundle by calling one hour before the 14 day advance purchase deadline. Also try airline websites. For more money saving suggestions, read the "Bargain Travel Handbook" from Travel Easy Publishing (in Sources chapter.)

Electronic ticketing can be convenient for you and the airline, if nothing goes wrong. However, if your flight is cancelled or seriously delayed, you won't have a paper ticket which could easily be endorsed to another airline. You would have to get to the ticket counter of the original airline and try to obtain a paper ticket to use on another line. The ticket agent may not be happy about you jumping ship, and there could be some delay. If there are many planes per day on your route, and you don't have to arrive by a certain time, electronic ticketing may be fine. Otherwise, it is probably safer to go to a travel agent to pay for your ticket and receive it on the spot. Then, if your flight is cancelled or repeatedly delayed, you can go to a phone and make a reservation on another flight. If you are not checking luggage, you can usually go directly to the gate.

To save money on meals, here are some suggestions. If your hotel includes a buffet breakfast in the room rate, you can tank up and then skip lunch. A small, quick snack in the afternoon can hold you until dinner. The time you saved by not having a sit-down lunch can be used for sightseeing. If breakfast was lighter, a few deli items make an inexpensive lunch. In small towns, you may need to pick these up before the stores close at noon. Larger cities usually have supermarkets.

If your hotel provides only coffee or tea, pick up bakery items the day before, so you can have breakfast in your room. If the hotel charges too much for breakfast, go elsewhere. In France, for example, you can pick up something at a bakery which is much better than what you would get at the hotel, and take it to a bar to enjoy along with your café au lait.

Sometimes it makes sense to have a breakfast snack on the run. We wanted to take an early boat from Mykonos to Delos, so we took our bakery items on board, along with hot tea which we bought at a café near the dock. Another time, we wanted to visit Ephesus early in the morning before it got hot. We nibbled on crackers and dried fruit while touring the site, and were able to finish the tour by 11:15, and then have an early lunch.

If you require a sit-down lunch, a cafeteria is a time and money saver, if the line is not long. Museums and department stores often have them. If the line is long, you might have to rely on your supply of nuts and dried fruit instead. When I'm trying to cram as much sightseeing into the day as possible, I prefer to pick up quick snacks from street vendors, and keep moving, rather than spend an hour or two on a restaurant lunch. I'd rather spend my time and money on a nice, relaxing dinner after the tourist sites close. However, if you are in a place where all the sites are closed for a two hour lunch, you may as well relax then.

For dinner, I ask the locals where they eat, and try to avoid the expensive tourist places. Some towns exist only for tourists, and the restaurants take advantage of the captive audience. See the sights as quickly as possible, and move on.

One question people often ask is "Should I rent a car?" Here are some factors to consider. If you are visiting major cities, you will save money and your sanity by relying on public transit. A car is not worth all the traffic and parking problems. However, if you are traveling about the countryside, a car can allow you to visit so many more places each week that it will actually make your money go farther, especially if there are two or more persons. If your vacation involves both types of places, you can try to get a hotel with parking on the outskirts of the city, on a bus or train line to the city center.

I have driven in many of the large cities in Europe, and I have a word of advice. That word is "Sunday." The business traffic is absent, and driving is easier than during the week, relatively speaking. You still may not be able to park near the sites that are open, but you can cover a lot of territory and get a good look at many building exteriors, landmarks and outlying neighborhoods. A "Sunday Driving" day can be a good complement to your weekday sightseeing. If you don't want to drive in unfamiliar territory, consider hiring a car with driver for the day. We did this one Sunday in Istanbul for less than it would have cost to rent just the car from an agency. Sunday is also a good day to pick up your rental car and try to find your way out of a city.

I've gotten the best prices on rental cars by renting them on the spot from a small, local agency. If I have concerns about the availability of certain features such as air conditioning and a secure luggage compartment, I reserve in advance, checking around for the best price. I sometimes give the travel agent who issues my airline ticket the opportunity to quote a rental car rate, but none has ever been able to match the rate I negotiated on my own. I pay with a credit card which covers the collision damage deductible, so I don't pay extra for the agency's waiver.

With all these money saving tips, you may now be thinking of a longer vacation. Wonderful! There are just a few little details remaining if you are going to leave home for more than a month. You will need to prepay utility and other bills, or arrange to have them paid automatically from your bank account. This applies especially to the credit cards you will use on your trip. Making twice the minimum payment one month will not absolve you from having to make the minimum payment the next month. Pay your entire balance plus enough to cover all but the last month of your trip, or make special arrangements with your bank.

If you don't want a house-sitter, consider putting your house in dormant mode, but don't just flip off the main circuit breaker as you leave. One guy did that, forgetting that his refrigerator wasn't empty. Yuck! Give away all perishables, and clean the refrigerator before you leave. With the electricity and gas turned off, there will be less worry about interior fire. It is most important that you turn off the water supply to the washing machine. The hoses can break under pressure, which usually seems to happen when people are away. My sister was house-sitting for my grandmother, and a hose broke while she was at work, flooding the house and ruining the carpet. The best long-term solution is to install the two-hose, one-lever shut-off valve. In any case, try to get in the habit of turning off the supply after each washload. At least do it before your trip.

Put small valuables in a safe deposit box and place larger ones in a big safe or with a trusted friend. The less you worry about the things at home, the more you can relax on your trip. Preparing for a trip may be a lot of work, but it pays off. When you are seated on the airplane, it's good to know that everything at home is taken care of, and nearly everything you are likely to need for your trip is in that little bag at your feet.

Whether you are traveling for business or pleasure, try to be good to yourself by getting enough sleep and healthy food. On long trips, I try to schedule one day a week for rest. If you are traveling on business, perhaps you can add a couple of days at the end for a mini vacation, visiting museums or whatever you like to do. Even if you are not a recreational shopper, you should buy a little gift for yourself, a souvenir of your trip which you will use often, such as a wallet or pair of earrings. Of course, the best gift is a trip with few stressful moments and many memorable ones. I hope this book will help you to have many such trips. Bons Voyages!

Chapter Twenty

OH WHERE, OH WHERE

Sources for Equipment and Information

AAA Global Currency   877-233-9234
aaa.com

Briggs and Riley   888-HMB BAGS
P.O.B. 3169, 102 Princeton Avenue
Half Moon Bay, CA 94019
Carry-On Tote no. 1130 and many other bags,
all with lifetime warranty

Do's and Taboos Around the World
edited by Robert E. Axtell
John Wiley and Sons, 1993

Overland Equipment   530-894-5605
2145 Park Avenue
Chico, CA 95928
Backpacks, Waistpacks, Duffels, etc.

Travel Easy   650-529-0282
1259 El Camino Real, no. 111
Menlo Park, CA 94025
travelsupercenter.com
Lightweight Carry-On and
Bargain Travel Handbook

TravelSmith   800-950-1600
60 Leveroni Court
Novato, CA 94949
travelsmith.com
Clothing and Accessories

Tumi, Inc.   800-322-TUMI
1001 Durham Avenue,
South Plainfield, NJ 07080
Large collection of Carry-Ons,
expensive

U.S. Customs Service
POB 7118
Washington, DC 20044
"Know Before You Go"

COPY THIS FORM
TO ORDER BOOKS

Please send IT'S IN THE BAG to:

Name:

Address:

City:

State: Zip:

Quantity desired:

Price per book $11.95 U.S.

Sales tax for California Addresses $0.90 per book

Packing and Shipping to U.S. Addresses $2.00
Order two or more to same address and we'll pay
to pack and ship by standard mail!
Priority Mail is $4.00 for up to four books.

Inquire about larger quantity discounts and
international shipping.

Please send check or money order to:

Château Publishing
P.O. Box 2401
Nevada City, CA 95959